The Glass Puddle

Sujatha Menon

The Glass Puddle
© Sujatha Menon

First Edition 2021

Sujatha Menon has asserted her authorship and given her permission
to Dempsey & Windle for these poems to be published here.

Front cover design by Sujatha Menon and Paul Windridge.

Published by Dempsey & Windle under their VOLE imprint

15 Rosetrees
Guildford
Surrey
GU1 2HS
UK
01483 571164
dempseyandwindle.com

British Library Cataloguing-in-Publication Data

A catalogue record for this book is available from the British Library

ISBN: 978-1-913329-54-9

Printed and bound in the UK

For Rafael, Eliza & Owen

*"Now I know how Joan of Arc felt
As the flames rose to her Roman nose
And her Walkman started to melt"*

Bigmouth Strikes Again
Steven Morrissey

Puddle I

I can splash through saris but not in skirts

Puddle II

I watered the lotus back to the mud

Puddle III

The ripples messed with my bindi

Puddle IV

I can reflect in Boli

Puddle V

My evaporation left a turmeric stain

Puddle VI

Now I rain like a monsoon in Mayfair

I

I can splash through saris but not in skirts

Exotica

They await me
at the end of a long swollen road
hemmed in by the Western Ghats;
reborn on Royal Enfields
strewn with garlands of jasmine
and red tinsel, hoping to serenade me
along the last few miles
to grandmother's house
on the edge
of a lazy snake-charmed village.

It is a place that hangs in the clouds
yet is equally of the earth,
ferrous red and cracked into lines of ants.
At the end of the old stone kitchen
is a well with a thousand silver fish
and a stove over which many stories have
been boiled into their milky essence,
poured into cups of cardamom chai
and given freely to visitors
who have come to see the
English-not-English
girl with the fringe.

Between the front of the house
and the back, a phantom limbed
veranda. You can sit here and drink
the monsoon as it drips down
from the thatch, poised like a
Hummingbird between heaven and hell;
that love-hate kiss you give to the homeland.

I circled around these shiny morsels today,
perched on a bench,
in the middle of England.

The Gaze

It was an Indian summer
in Wigan, a fragrant afternoon.
Mother's orange Frangipani sari
trailed like a peacock's tail
in the apple blossom,
showered down in reverence
to cushion her steps.
I had been collected from school,
bottle-green and chubby
splashing through the petals
as we walked home.

Twenty years later
I developed a plume
soaked in violet and gold,
and mosaiced in confetti
cast from soft hands.

Twenty years later
I sit and stroke each feather,
the orange ones now almost red

all eyes in the past,
all eyes looking back,
all eyes fanned wide,

gazing at the girl
who blazed into a woman.

Dark Star

I am a fire-worker
I swallow flames
I trap light in my gut
In my heart
In my veins
I transform light into
darkness
I blackluminesce
I am a fire-worker
I swallow flames

Commitment

You never did
give me a
stickin' out ring.
So I bought one
for 99p
in the Claire's Accessories sale.

I slipped it beneath
the wedding band
I never wore,
and finally
fell in love with myself.

Sari Safari

It's wedding season
and arranged love
is in the air!

The earrings of the neighbour
who wasn't invited, hang like the chandeliers
on Harley Street dripping with excess rent.

The ladies who *have* been invited
form a silk rainbow around
the bride about to bucklebend
from her weight in gold.

She has not far to walk to the heavenly stage
which I imagine would actually feel like heaven
if it weren't hooked up to twenty televisions
and ten thousand eyes outside (not hyperbole).

The ceremony is short and hypnotic —
filled with such fire and grace
I thought I had been standing there
for a lifetime, or at least India Time
which is the time zone
my husband says I operate in.

I had been 'delayed' for my own wedding too,
but have never been as unpunctual to anything
as my own life, crawling through my 40's
like I did in my first egg and spoon race
and disqualified for making a false start.

I like to call it IMT Time or
in-my-own-time
because at least that sounds like
I have some control over the matter,
which of course I don't;
because once the call of the bride
arrives...

so does the wild dance of the
sari-safari, sandals, bangles and scandals.
And clocks turned to the wall.

Cousins

It has a colossal trunk,
dry-wrinkled and crusty baked;
so old, the cracks are aged
with the royal pelt
of moss and lichen.

My elephantine tree
swings wild in the wind,
and I am blown
into the Motherland
on the back of a
blue-billed bird
that rides on the tusk
of this wise mammal's head.

My skin still feels England;
a wetsuit, shy and clinging
but it won't save me from the heat
under the cotton trees, or the
coconut that might split my skull.

It is a thin layer of rubber
that separates you from me.
Me trapped on the inside,
you repelled on the outside,

a dark impermeable membrane
that stretches for miles
but could easily rip raw
when we smell the jasmine in the Malabar breeze,

see the baby elephant queuing in the traffic,
hear the ring of the temple bell by the sea,
feel the first drop of monsoon after the relentless fire,
and devour the mangos
we both call home.

Trench Coat

March wanted to march:
restless and frothing
tiny white flowers into corners
and dark spaces. But it had only just
turned February, and that will
between sleep and wake
was not yet ready to battle
or acquiesce to anything
plump or frilly.

I too wandered in a
kind of limbo, suspended
between death and
fruiting,
with all the turmoil of
something trying to hatch
through fragility into
places that could easily break me.

The catkins hung from the bare bones
of trees, like quarter notes waiting
for the wind to play their melody,
but the birds arrived first —
a discord of creaking doors,
tin whistles,
squeaking hinges
and bud-busting drills.

Mole hills humped
with snow
melted in the sun,
sticky and pudding-like —
and from across the field
a ferocious frosty breath
roaring past an allotment fire.
Perhaps from the ashes of an
old ice-dragon.

Spring was not here yet, but
neither was the monsoon.

Sea Stacks

~~Intermediate~~
~~Betwixt~~
~~Midway~~
~~Halfway~~
~~Between~~
Centred
~~Connecting~~
~~Joining~~
~~Equidistant~~
~~Transition~~
~~Limbo~~
~~~~~~~~~

Keranut Song

Keranut girl
mouthful of pearls,
crushing fine lines
she can never unlearn.
Burberry on the inside,
Barbour on the outside,
all banyan in the middle.

Keranut girl
in her shell-suit of plaid,
inside, her skin is tattered and frayed.
Burberry on the inside,
Barbour on the outside,
all banyan in the middle.

Keranut girl
clip-clops like a horse;
a trojan-in-waiting
licks its obstacle course.
Burberry on the inside,
Barbour on the outside,
all banyan in the middle.

Keranut girl
tenderly farts.

Chips x 3 Ways

Amma whispers pukka prayers,
that set sail through generations.
I think this is why Dad orders
omelette and chips
when we go to Shimla Palace.
And why Mum went for a McDonald's
veggie burger and fries for her birthday
instead of being taken to King Baba
or The Indian Queen;
the reason you can't see
my forehead or my long, curly name.
Oh and I prefer instant coffee,
black no sugar — no masala, no chai.

Godlessing

On my way to nowhere,
just before I came to the
old stone bridge,
the sky shivered
grey on my right
while to the left
the sun continued
to boil the sky blue.

Somewhere was a place
where light and darkness
kissed each one of my cheeks as
an excuse not to meet each other.

I realised
I had also wandered into
a contentment
that was neither
happy or sad —
snug in a space
between forces
that could easily kill each other;
Durga on downtime
without her sword.

The Magic Roundabout

Every trip out into the melt
is like Russian Roulette
played with a mala bead.

The spinning wheel
of the magic roundabout
is a whirl of
baby elephants
rickshaws
bikes
scooters
cars
crows
vegetable sellers
stray dogs and —
bright hallucinogenic lorries
all within an inch of death
from each other.

There is a man cradled
on the edge
of a fresh twenty storey high rise
having a nap on a ledge as thin as his leg.
If he's still there in thirty minutes
he will continue to work
on the spray of wires
which might offer
a less messy end.

On the windowsill
overlooking the sleeping suicide,
two pigeons,
happy and inseparable
and always there when we return
to this house from home.

Being as free as birds
they are not knifed to the edge
by penury,
but are perfectly balanced in life
as on the ledge.

I've never had to visit
that brink either.
My circus was the tightrope
tied between two retreating worlds
with a safety net of
pride and privilege.
But I was becoming heavy...

India has given the world
so many amazing things,
but health & safety
aint one of 'em.

Solstice

The first bite of winter
arrives like a cold-blooded
vampire starving for my neck.
And a darkness
that I have come to call home,
cloaks the light.

I switch on a lamp
and stir
my bubbling stew
laced with wine and the
crosses of cloves;
one hand on the stove,
the other turning each bulb
of the garlic rosary
that hangs
from the full blood moon.

Dominatrix

The Snow Queen has been...
Her tears congealed
into snowdrops not ready to spring.

Frosted panes of ice lie shattered
along the edges of the lane where
her pale shadow skated by,
blowing glass puddles
that form reluctantly in her wake,
their surface as cracked as
cold morning lips.

Her final act is to pull an invisible
rug from beneath my feet.
And I am forced to kiss hers.

Kickin' Kali

She opened her mouth
Devoured the town
The wrath of Kali
Blew my house down

Ten thousand tongues
Flickered like flames
Licked at my wounds
Again and again

The dance of old endings
And of new beginnings

Again and again...

Hex

Last night
the stars combusted;
each one of their five points
smoking jet trails
down to the sea.

Above the water
they rehang in
gaseous ghostly clouds,
gull studded,
wings flicker
in and out of view.

Trapped between layers
of sky, mist, sea and land,
I shiver and harden
into a spell,
waiting to be discovered
by a magician's hand.

Chant for Health & Safety

I slipped through a slit with my first aid kit
no-bandage-or-plasters-or-shame in it.
CONTENTS: ink, vinyl, coffee,
a flower, bubblebath, frankincense,
x1 small bottle of 'drink me', Kali doll.

I slipped through a slit with my first aid kit
no-identity-number-or-claim on it.
PLACE OF MANUFACTURE: Watery Lane (see p61).

I slipped through a slit with my first aid kit
no-table-or-booklet-or-blame on it.
INSTRUCTIONS: follow gut.

Black Grapes

Deepti's braids dripped
full fat ink,
coiled thick and hung
like grapes.

At night, her fruitfall
bounced in the mirror,
leaked from pale breasts
and down the wave
of her spine
knotted and gnarled
from sitting too straight
in a wild wonky world.

In her mind, ten fingers
glide to ride the swell
of each curl pooled
at the waist.

There is another life
that runs loose
through long hair,
but how to catch it
when you can't even
pick up the brush.

Strangers

A new auntie was due to visit in the afternoon;
new because aunties are mass produced
in Little India.
Just like you are likely to be gallstoned
for being female, fat and forty,
you qualify to be an auntie
if you add Indian on to that list.
If you bring boli or laddoo
you may even be promoted
to *amma* or mother.

The one that arrived at 12pm,
early enough to snatch away my dinner,
looked like she had perfected this trick
into a profession — a dinnermonger
with tremendous teeth
that protruded like tuning forks
or parrot claws used to manipulate
food.

My sister was three years old
when auntie picked her up,
little fingers trying to press
down each key
or toe, depending on which way
you looked at it.

Not knowing how to blush,
everyone moved swiftly
to the dining room hoping
the little girl would be released
for proper food.

When it was time to leave
everyone blocked the front door
exchanging last minute gossip
that turned into major news.

Our kid was sent
like a wound-up toy
to kiss auntie goodbye,
and to disperse the crowd.

II

I watered the lotus back to the mud

Houdinii

Through a crack
in the grey plastic drain
appeared a small yellow flower.
Not a glossy buttercup
or a frilly dandelion
but an 'unknown'
overdressed for the party.

I marvelled at how it had escaped
through such a fine gap
and so labelled her Houdinii
spelt with two i's
because they looked like
two stamens.

Petals intact
and now with a name,
I plucked her out of the plastic
and pressed her between the pages
of my yoga magazine.

Superpowers

Did you know that butterflies
can taste with their feet?
Well I can see with my gut.

Did you know that a snake
can smell with its tongue?
Well I can touch with my eyes.

Did you know that some frogs
can hear with their mouth?
Well I can taste the whole world
with my mind.

Wildflowers

God how we screamed,
scribbling sacrilege
in neat handwriting
on Sunday School scrawl.

Tearing through
the churchyard
like rogue violets streaking
across the neglected grass,
we recongregate
in the telephone box
for Sado Scrabble
with the operator.

It's true I was a wild child,
and the flower side of me
was a bit ragged
around the edges too.
But I had learned to
gild my petals in
a kind of lilac-silver
to deflect the colour
in my name.

And so I roamed barefoot
amongst the daisies, foxgloves,
cowslip and nettle,
not knowing
all the while
I was lining in a
leaf of gold.

Full Bloom

Red Calla Lily:
a brimful display
of mid-life crisis.
Her George
and Mildred
conjoined,
lovingly locked
in eternal disgrace.

Snowbells

If I could pick you a flower,
I would make a snowdrop
lined in ultra-violet.
Pollen-pots crammed
with the grains of ground gun.
It has taken elastic long years
to burst open to life,
and I'm still not sure
where my sparks will fly
or if I'll just set myself on fire.

Jasmine

Yin and yang
yang and yin
ylang-ylang smells like jasmine.
Jasmine is condensed milk
of the moon that sleeps
all day in the sea,
turning and churning
white morning waters
in lacto-galactic bloom.

Yang and yin
yin and yang
ylang-ylang smells like jasmine,
that flakes from a star
or a cold lunar scar,
hung high by hot hands
in stale garlands of light,
above bananas and gourds
okra and cloves,
like a pearl-powered jubilee.

Yin and ylang
ylang and yin
are the
top notes
heart notes
base notes
of a song
I dreamt into a flower.

Roses & Peonies

A peony is a shaggy rose,
a Margo to a Lilibet,
less royal but more regal
and more cousin than sister.
Being sweeter and less peppery
than a rose, and only available
at certain times of year,
the peony is a seasonal nectar
flowing freely around high tea
at the allotment where it tumbles
over Collin's cauliflowers
as if to soften his UKIP
leanings to the soil.
He shows me his big bad brassica
(to prove he knows how it's done).
I show him my horror.
And then we both squabble about the peony
and if its acting like weeds.

Bird of Paradise

an exotic flower,
an exquisite bird,
a difficult pose.

When bent out of shape
I am still so beautiful;

torn petal,
dislocated wing.

When bent out of shape
I am an exotic pose,
a torn flower,
an exquisite petal,
a difficult bird
with a dislocated wing.

Lotus

I think they've got it all wrong;
the gurus with their soft petal hands
oiled in the grease of scandal-wood,
sliding the easy girls up from the filth.

Lie lo, lie lo, lie lo-lo-lotus

I think they've got it all wrong.
The lotus should return to the mud,
to soothe its stalk and drip its crown
in earth's healing paste.

Lie lo, lie lo, lie lo-lo-lotus

I've never cared much for the sun,
preferring to play and later drink in cellars
beneath where things grow to the light,
and shine up your skirt
as you reach high for salvation.

Here's a chant you can use:

Lie lo, lie lo, lie lo-lo-lotus
Lie lo, lie lo, lie lo-lo-lotus,
you gotta rock 'n'roll in the mud
tight as a bud

Stay lo, stay lo, stay lo-lo-lotus...

Plantation

Cricket song, pitchy
and as garrulous
as the pineapples prickling
under the moon.

So much unsaid,
driving through the yellow
pines sugaring inside,
to a doorway
where a tiger once ate
from the palms of grandfathers
squared.

Now, just the front of the house remains,
like a needle lost
in a sprawling rubber estate
in which we now stood waiting
for the sun to shine its secrets
and through the saris
of old aunts splashing like children
in the fish fried river.

I only dipped my toes in
to avoid electrocution —
from a body wired
by a journey
backwards
forwards
across
and around
the slip of time,
dripping like the toddy
sugaring inside the trees;
the same trees
that had made the
soles of my feet.

I now knew where I came from.
I now knew
that roots could grow shoes.

Forget-me-nots

Tiny daggers of blue
remember to burst
into the light
of your brand new day.
Even traumas have colours.

Buttercups

I held a buttercup
beneath my double chin.
It shone
a jaundiced thought
across my seeping skin.
Blood
Pus
and antibiotics.
Just like
milk.
Just like
butter.

Violet

Morning mass,
everywhere!
an overnight decision —
purplesong
pursed in mouthfuls,
ready to serenade the bride
that doesn't arrive.

I wonder how many times
these flowers have been forsaken,
or do they just love an excuse
to come up
to kiss my eyes.

Daisy Chain

We hang around
each other's neck,
where there is
no beginning
nor an end.
Choking in the sunshine.

Hydra (or Hydrangea?)

Nine stars above the steeple
and six minutes in,
the curse was aligned,
just like the rubber yogi
had said back in the ashram
filled with the roar of lions.

That night was just an ordinary night;
cooking, reading, watching TV.
I took a bath with a new scented soap
and dyed my hair the colour of sleep when
a nightmare arrives but you are still awake
planning to cook your head in the oven,
and then wash it down with red wine from
no region in France.

At six minutes past the hour
I found I had food to sculpt
a song to slake
words to clear
French to fry
a class to carve
paintings to seal

all with a self-imposed deadline
of now.

A dead line
is a curse aligned,
though you all say it is a blessing.

The Nightgarden

These particular flowers
bloomed in the doom;
Coco Mademoiselles
spraying all things crawling
under the moon.

This process of silversynthesis
lit whole cities,
while I lay pretend sleeping
with a pen-torch
under a constantly collapsing
planetarium.

I still wake early
with star-gritted eyes,
searching for clues in
the mattress —
a beam burnt
through the bed,
a Little Dipper
in the duvet,
a black hole
where my head disappeared
last night.

The Dandelion's Clock

Its skeleton is a called a clock.
In ten puffs time, its ribs will float

over a sea of blades thrashing green.
Once settled, each will grow a fine-toothed mane
once again

and roar amongst the daisies and the daffs
because a dandelion doesn't self-identify as weeds.

His power is herbal, magical, medicinal,
named from the round mouth of France:

dent-de-lion, seeded down to one word
like a chain of whispers blown to the wind

like so many of our names, blown to the wind.
How long until we lose all our teeth?

III

The ripples messed with my bindi

Rice

Rice.
Shoved under the carpet
with the peas,
and down it goes
through the open top of the piano,
sticky keys.
Rice and yoghurt
all over my mouth and cheeks,
stuck behind the sofa
and in the gap between my teeth.
Boiled white gum
smeared along paper
when we ran out of glue —
split, ground or fried
into different foods.
A handful hidden under half a soggy poppadum.
Another handful arranged under the half-eaten salad.
Another handful thrown back in my face
as I remembered in a lunch meeting.
As I choked on the Maki sushi
and couldn't stop giggling.

Malice

You need special shoes
to latch across the rocks.
It's the only way to
chase the slippery edge
of the Solent
that rabbles out from the bay.

Glassy pools filled with the
juice of emeralds
trap your gaze,
sucking eyes
from toes
that forget they are
not barnacles.

So you dive in
to break the fall,
green spells
swimming through
scratched lips,
shrinking to the size
of a periwinkle

to wake up
in the bathtub,
big toe stuck up the tap
and all dreams
of the island
swirling
down
the
plug
hole.

Wonderland

Today I walked to the edge
of town where the village green
had expanded overnight;
the old pillar box shrivelled
to a small red mouth
with attitude, like punk post
spitting out letters.

What sort of witchery was this?

The same that had been cast
on the tin of Quality Street
to the delight of Celebrations
celebrating O' Purple Ones
being taken down a size
until they realised
they had been too.

The fate of vinyl was the worst;
that shiny spiral of black magic
disappeared into a puff of air,
dispersing through invisible
wires attached to something
as small and bright as a square
of gold leafed chocolate.

I wondered if my mind had withered
from outsourcing movement to
tea bags, fob keys and online
everything, or was it swollen with data
crammed tight to the bone.

Being five foot one
with nowhere to grow,
I imagined my head like a Bonsai
injected with steroids,
then walked back
to the centre of town.

Kanyakumari

At the southernmost tip
of Kerala, 321 kilometres
from the Cardamom Hills,
between the Indian Ocean
Arabian sea and
Bay of Bengal,
amongst a confluence
of tourists —
you will find her.

Forsaken here
on her wedding day,
the virgin goddess roams
and combs the shores
for tiny uncooked pebbles
of rice that were going to feed
at least five thousand.

The grains have now turned to stone;
saltrocks precipitated from tears
which she spends the rest of eternity collecting.

As this is also a place where
the sun and moon hang together,
I give her a hand, stuffing
some of the sadness into my pocket.

When I get home
where she is known as
Cape Comorin (so don't know her at all)
I place the pebbles
in the pond scaping the garden,
hoping to one day see her
rise up through the rain.

Watery Lane

Could I swim down Watery Lane?
Yes, but not very well.
My style is called: 'The Joan Collins'
fully made-up with
a matching martini-fag hand;
head sliding along
like a plastic swan
at a carnival.

I don't wear much makeup anymore
or smoke, but I do like a glass of wine
which I once helped to make
in an orchard in Texas,
bursting grapes with my corns
and claws which I grew during
school from wearing tiny fashion-shoes
and even tighter clothes under my uniform.
So I did a good job with the grapes.

I am apparently eighty percent water
so only twenty percent of me
actually needs to swim which
makes things a bit easier
as I'm down
to my last
ten percent
and no
one
can
save
me.

Aqueduct

Neyyar Dam: reimagined...

Twelve demi loops
weave in and out of love,
sewn through the river
in gradients of green;
seabows — salty and stained
by the sap of minerals ground
to a grain by a good lashing
from the sea.

Where was its head and its wings?

Pulled underneath
by boggy eyes, ducts clogged
with splinters of cement,
aqua filed and pricking
tiny orange fish that had
escaped its scale-slit blades.

I wanted to thread myself
into her stubborn tail,
to ride the feeling
of high and heavy,
be part of the course
to the other side,
delivering plenty.

Silver Bells

Half Old Curiosity Shop,
half palace museum,
The Emporium offered an
emerald mint tea
poured from a silver teapot.

This fine liquid coolant
was a medicine for my
delicate English hands, burnt
from the rupees roasting
in my pocket.

Even more fiery
was a huge golden statue
of the ten-armed Kali
surrounded by flames
that licked my purse.

I thought of all the ways
I could take her back
home to Leamington Spa,
where I imagined her sizzling
next to Queen Victoria,
at the bottom of The Parade.

But she was too fabulous to carry
and too big to fit into the miniature
minds that won't give back
the crown jewels.

I picked a tinkling silver anklet
instead, so that I might remember
the chains around the ankles
of my ancestors
every time I took a step away
from this once trampled land.

Gold

Loneliness
is a steel water trough
in the centre of a big empty field.
Like the existence of just a single object
in the middle of the middle floor
in the Tate Modern

or a Duchamp
sneaked into a public space
for a double-entendre
or just a laugh.

I stand invisible,
centre-stage
in the playground,
only seen when it's time
to be struck for leaking
visibly brown.

But still I shine
in my own darkness,

and they hate it.

SOS

It never
occurred to me
that out of the
8 billion souls
on this
planet,
mine
would find
yours,
and yours
would
save mine.

Light Seeds

Freshly fluffed soil
waits neatly in a square.
The allotment has shivered
off its cold.

A mixed bag of
fingers now poke
it back to life, warm
and drilling
light seeds
that will respond
in the dark,
unlock their code
and escape into a gut.

Here they will blend
with instinct and
energise a finger to
prod traditions that are
stony dead;
that have buried us alive
because we are the same
colour as the earth.

Crème Brûlée (Ve)

My mother's first language
is not English.
Which is why she thinks
my father has a 'soft corner'
for their cat.

I don't have any undiagnosed
lumps or bumps
so am already tender inside
but with edges torched
into a brittle battle
that crack with every
tap, tap, tap
of fingers poking into nooks
collapsing from the ooze.

If I had grown inside a chewy skin
my corners may have softened
instead of crumbling.
Just like mother said,
whose first language
is not English.

Ritual

But you have such a beautiful name!

10-Sue-jath-a
9-Su-jar-ther
8-Suj-arthur
7-Sushana (??)
6-Sue-jeeta
5-Suj-attta
4-Sujar-the
3-Sujarva (cockney)
2-Sujar-thar (close)
1-Suj-utha

Time up:
Just Su —
without an e.

Black Ice

I slipped
and fell
into a darkness
I could not
see.

Anxiety

Bed
Savasana
Durga mantra
Pray
She leaves you
Her weapons...

Intersection

I am not homeless.
I have many fixed abodes,
including a permanent one at
the railway station:
'mind the gap
mind the gap
please mind the gap'.

The gap gapes
a soft fontanelle,
raw worlds unfused
but enough flesh to mesh
me a bed where I sleep
with no destination.

Home

When
your body
becomes a
sofa
for your sister's fungal feet
your mother's nodding off head
your cat's fat belly
and your father's
Remote
Control.

Snow White & The Seven Devis

It took many cracked years to look in the mirror
and see that I was queen of my darkness,
and that I didn't need seven dwarfs or a prince
to save me from the poison that whitewashed the world.

I am the seven Devis!
And between us
we have 80 arms
600 eyes
and a tongue that can whip you
up into a fairy tail,
though a fairy doesn't have a tail,
it has wings
which are just a delicate way
of having more arms.

Fairness Cream

A flamingo's poo is not pink,
yet its feathers are, painted
by algae and shrimp.
You can also turn yellow or orange
from eating too many carrots.
Someone died doing so in 1972.
Imagine, only a year after my birth
a woman overdosed on carrots.
But I've never spotted an orange rabbit — not one,
though I've seen many white elephants

DENIAL denial DENial
doesn't look pretty in any colour.

Centifeet

When the ground fell
beneath me
I stood
on my own ten feet
and put on
ALL my sparkly
shoes.

IV

I can reflect in Boli

Chamundi Hill Palace

It lay dreaming of England
on the nib of a mountain
high in swirl of the
Malabar clouds.

The old Mercedes
was having none of it.
After all, it wasn't a bloody packhorse.
Its proper job was to glide us
through the city to places
like the Taj. The *Royal* Taj.

The 'Silver Lady'
did everything she could
to protest in the only way she knew how:
spluttering, jerking, collapsing on her
back wheels spinning, on a path
rutted and roughshod,
presumably from the many
metal Trojans before us.

Eventually, a collective sigh opened
the gates just as the light was dimming
and we entered a kingdom
balanced on a pinhead
or somebody's thumb.

Sleep came in a tree house
with an electric socket
skilfully camouflaged in the trunk.
If you stuck your head out
of its painted yellow hole
you could see the edge of your
life and beyond. The swaying chain
of sticks that hemmed us all in
also gave little reassurance.

Dotted across the quilted garden,
bright paper-machéd figures
of gods, goddesses, lions, monkeys
and James Bond
until you reached the long
whitewashed hall with a floor so shiny
it could have easily been a swimming pool
#riskhazard No.2

Next to the hall was a house
where they could have filmed
the Indian version of
Fawlty Towers,
complete with a stuffed tiger
that used to be a pet.

But my favourite place
was the divan swing
where I sat like Sita
on the devil's trapeze
rocking high into the heavens.
I could have been the entertainment.

That evening, after dinner
on a banana leaf curling
off a dishcloth,
it occurred to me
that I wasn't in a palace at all,
but in a castle stacked
on a thousand winged elephants.

Pudding Bag Lane

Pudding Bag Lane:
there are five in England —
all cul-de-sacs.

I grew up near such a sac
in Thurlaston, Warwickshire.
But it wasn't called Pudding Bag Lane
because it was a dead end...

A pudding bag is a cloth pouch
in which an uncooked pudding
is boiled, so this is a place where
people once baked in a circle;
an enclosed pocket of industrious
storytelling
dream-making
soul-bearing and
past-sharing;
histories spooled
from the tongue
and intricately laced into the
cloth of the pudding bag.

Of course, this is all untrue.
But it is a real story.

Silverfish

The needle darts
in and out of the herringbone
like a silverfish in the carpet
flashing Morse code to
save the button.

Its fine tipped sting
once picked out
a long boat-of-a-splinter
and left its poison
to bathe in the excavation.

Such a needle was also used
to pierce my sister's little ears
and my mother's nose —
the old-fashioned Indian way

but me and my blood-sister
boiled it three times
before we pressed our
sixteen-year-old thumbs together
and scratched our name
across the other's wrist.

Also, at that time, a habit
of sewing my school skirt so tight
I had to walk sideways up the stairs.
This brings me to the clothes
my mother stitched onto my dollies
which I had to cut off
before I put them to bed.

This is what happens when you squint
through the eye of a needle!

81

No. 12 Eccleston Street

The ambulance was ready —
flashing bright orange
flowers and nylon, a bumpy ride
from hospitality above
to clinic below
in the days you could visit doctors
almost in pyjamas.

There were options:

Shoot through the big door
and cause patients,
or take a first right into
the waiting room where we
would eat dinner
in about six hours' time.

But I usually took a second right
into the room with
the glowing purple antiseptic,
a colour so magical
it would tow me
into another world.

When I returned from my rounds
I'd visit 'Auntie Eva' who'd serve brown files
through the hatch from the kitchen
and me a packet of Polos, which is probably why
I now have a hole in the middle of each tooth.

Next stop — past the storehouse of
samosas, spices and milk sweets —
the outside toilet
where patients pissed out smoke;
I could see it leaking through
the keyhole.
No wonder they needed to see my dad

sitting behind his desk with a sign
which said *no smoking*
and a drawer full of fags

and mum's set off the fire alarm again
with masala fish-fry.

The ambulance was ready.

Time Machine

Zero to forty-nine in three seconds.
Like nought to a hundred,
foot knifed to the pedal,
except I'm not a Ferrari or a Bugatti
but a Citroën CV6 that girlfriends
of guitarists used to drive into
school and straight back out again.

My vehicle has a drinks cabinet
and an ashtray spitting out
lipsticked stubs like
the ends of crap jokes.
In the wing mirror,
denial dressed in funeral black
that nearly killed me.
I never look at the rear view
in case I catch a self
I have run over,
left behind,
fly-tipped at forty.

Where to look then
except into
the faux-lined interior,
its seams hardened
with age
and from resistance to
forces trapped
in its trojan tank

searching for the slow lane,
the stop sign,
the red light.

Teen Spirit

Spirals in vinyl
etched by a witch's tooth
scratching screams
of 'yeah baby'
when you stick the needle in.

I made a devil's lounge
from bedsheets, beads and
magazines,
and ra-ra danced
in my Mardi Gras
whirling to the spell
of the Voodoo Child
that sent me
into a teenage spin

dancing before the
blue-tacked shrine
of Hendrix and
Le Bon.

Upstairs Downstairs

Mother left dinner at the top of the stairs
on a cracked *Wham* tray splitting George
and Andrew right down the middle.

Voluntarily imprisoned in my room
I feasted on a hunk of *Houses of the Holy*
and *Stairway to Heaven* with fingers raw
from stale air guitar.

Downstairs Amma was singing
in ribbons of raag that tied themselves
around the lotus feet of Sri Robert Plant.

Occasionally you could hear a lyric
that transformed into Indlish
as it escaped through the walls
to remind me in no uncertain terms
that I belonged downstairs as well as upstairs.

In later years I wrote songs such as:
Rockin' Rani
Bolly Parton
and *Grease*

What a difference a stair makes.

Sweet Sixteen

Pink gin
Bubblegum sin
Sweetness sinks down
to my gutter
I let my poison rise
I let my poison rise...

Brown Girl in the Ring

Pivot-pirouette
from foot to fist,
whole body whip
lashing to the tip —
hooked by the left,
jabbed by the right,
a tango of two halves
caught in a fight:

show me your motion
come on show me your motion
tra-la-la-la-la-la

from uppercut to Downward Dog
I trained my army
to slip, duck and slide,
to snake through the weave
of skin and hate
spilling bright from the corners
of shops, into the Black Holes of Balti —
then to the pub
punch drunk.

Black Swan

Nora's sweetshop
stuck to the top of the hill.
Here you could find many species
of sugar exhibited in jars
as well as animals —
wooden, plastic, inflatable
that hung from the ceiling
giving the impression you were
in *The Jungle Book* or
on Noah's Ark.

When the hill disappeared
and the shop shrunk
to the size of a Wendy house,
I remembered playing
Mowgli in the big ballet,
viewed through the
barrel ends of binoculars,
swinging from a beam.

Holy Cows

I went to India for a holiday when I was nine years old
and came home aged eleven.

In that sticky gap
I learned how to hide Mills & Boon
from evil nuns,
and how to roast them in their habits
when they found romance bristling
behind plain brown covers.
This was achieved by wearing black
patent winklepickers,
which was confusing
because the points were at the front
rather than on the heel
which would have made them slut-shoes and
relegated to the same cupboard as the slut-books.

Life is a misery
Everyone must stand in their own shoes

Near the school was a junction
where a mosque, church and temple
shared at least the same space
if not the same view —
this ethos was not extended up the road.

Just like a prayer you know I'll make you swear

My days as a little Hindu weirdo
tap dancing in the convent
were finally numbered when I began
to sing hymns from the Top 40.
This was more confusing than the winklepickers
because it ALL pointed in the wrong direction
which was down —
the bottom 10 to be exact.

90

And so I was put on a plane back to Lancashire,
just in time to head in the direction of
Madonna's pointy bra.

I hear you call my name and it feels like home
Just like a prayer your voice will take me there...

Camera Obscura

Prayers are kept in the darkroom,
lit by the triple flame of aarti
reflecting on frames
of ancestors and avatars.
Ten arms flicker in the corner of sight,
animated past death by fire,
and a sword is shining
on the alter — a funeral pyre,
where evil is slain and spiralled
up to salvation
in sandalwood smoked and sweet.

I once thought I saw
a sacrificial fish,
scales about to give up
its secrets from the sea.
But I had caught
a chink of wrapping
flashing its two-tone skin
now assigned forever to paper
the cracks of a
plastic cockroach sanctuary.

The breath of impending monsoon
warns the lamp —

which signals all-a-flicker
to black souls trapped
behind glass, framed and fuming

to get ready for the shot:

We kneel, we pray, we point our tongues.
We kneel, we pray, we click our teeth.
We kneel, we pray, we capture — no God
Om shanti, shanti, shanti...

Gravity

You can only see the wind
by the shake and sway
of trees, bending like a spoon
from the mind of Uri Geller.

What invisible force has
twisted me
out of shape
that I should bow and scrape
my knees along the boundary
of here and there:

Pudding and pilau
Chamomile and chai
Sari and skirt
Raag and rock
Fingers and fork
Life and death.

My Regeneration

I've lived a live wire,
ricocheted, swayed to a snake
juicing whole cloves, whole cities
squeezed
to their unholy waters —
but the street lights remain
glow-spot the stains
of monuments swallowed
to a pulp, paper-machéd
to an egg
that will never crack
or boil hard
any truth.

Show me your sunny side
And I will show you my shell.

Rock-a-bye Baby

My cot still breathes,
barely rocking in an upstairs hall
from the palms of trees fanning in the breeze
through slats that never shut.
'This was your cot!' grand uncle says
every time we travel five thousand miles
to see how he tends to our ghosts,
of which he is now one.
I still hang on the wall
in a little white dress and black strapped shoes,
with a tap dance of curls like Shirley Temple,
sitting nose-to-nose on the courtyard step
with my first guru called *Saint* —
as in Simon Templar.
He is also black and white
being a Border Collie,
and we are both very dusty.
His bones now lie beneath
a fragrant garden shrine
roofed in lemon leaves and red roses
that fleck the white marble
cool and snoring
behind a tiny iron gate.
Here, also,
the ashes of the ghosts that still rock
me to my dreams,
all fighting for space inside the body
I have come to call home,
waiting to fall onto a page or into a song
when I awake.

The Mermaid's Torso

'There's too much sparkle on your scales.
It's going to outshine your human side
which is already drowning'

This was coming from a seahorse
that didn't know what time of day it was
or that it wasn't half a horse.

The mermaid transferred the
pearlescent flecks
onto her burnt brown skin
that flashed a sea of lighthouses
to keep predators at bay,
the ones that wanted to cannibalise
her off the bone. But once the twinkle
was scraped off her tail,
it began to corrode and eat itself
like fish-eating gangrene.
She didn't care. Not a bit.
She was only half human after all.

Standard Deviation

Uncoordinated doesn't equal clumsy or graceless,
it just means they can't find you
by scratching their stupid beards.

By the time X has crossed Y
you are long gone,
out-out of your skin,
blazing borders, boundaries and barriers,
riding the trajectories that warn
of some excitement
that can't yet be contained.

I love how digits cling fast
to the edge, like the scum
of tarka dhal that curdles to the pan
foaming at the mouth, begging
to be skimmed by the silver spoon
once rammed down my throat.

Yes, I am a deviant, the new norm —
and this is why you can appreciate the curves
on a girl like me.

Parallel Lines

I stopped at the old stone hump,
a rainbow of cement
bridging leaving and going.
The railway track laddered away
in an astonishingly straight line
that passed beneath my feet
and for miles behind

to 1986 which was the year
I had hair that was not permitted
to deviate in any direction whatsoever
apart from down, towards the
rear curve of black stilettoes
I slipped on like Cinderella
outside the school gates.
From here, it was another
straight line to the pub
where you would never find Penelope
because she was always in the library
twirling her fingers across pages
and around long pieces of hair
so unbending,
her ears would slice through
on either side to ensure
not even a strand would kink
out of line.

I dreamt of having hair like Penelope.
It was the only time in my life
I desired such inflexibility,
in a world where a
spiral, coil or curl would shatter
my lineage and ascension into
science.
But I could only tame the wild for so long;
we didn't even have ghd's back then.
I ended up at art school,
in a rock 'n' roll band,
writing this poem;
expressing my double helix.

V

My evaporation left a turmeric stain

666

When people ask where
my place of birth is, I say 'Wales'
hoping they won't take it any further.
But then comes the 'whereabouts?'
to which I reply too loudly:
'The Arse End' (Newport).

Though lately I've been trying out
Twll Du which sounds exotic,
roughly means the same thing in Welsh
and, is the name of a place
I could easily be born into...

Deep in the bowels
of Snowdonia National Park,
the Devil's Kitchen hunches
ravenously over a lake.
Its great boulder of a bum
is split into two by a
long black crack — *Twll Du*.
Legend says that smoke rises
up through the crack
when Satan is cooking.
I didn't see any smoke
but I did see a large group
of students on a navigation course
getting completely lost.
Perhaps forces were messing
with their compass,
sending it wild and spinning
back in the direction of Newport.

I was spawned early
at The Royal Gwent Hospital
in a beastly coat of thick black hair.
It's the only time I've been early
in my whole life.

One day either side,
I would have been born
back in Wigan;
and there are no other
words to describe that.

Horrorscope

I used to think that a horoscope was used to map out
the scope of horror you might encounter in your life.

That it could name with bindipoint accuracy
the monsters hiding under your bed
or in an empty cot.

I imagined further, it could warn of earthquakes
and forecast with OS detail where the cracks
would form beneath your feet
so I might at least work on my splits
when two worlds flew apart.

A Libra born between the sun and the snow
I always tip towards the dark side,
this way, I can schmooze with the monsters
now grown below my king size,
run wild with their fear
that has come to define and release me.

Libra or libre,
tomayto, tomahto.

Turmeric Gold

If I were a mark
left in your memory,
I'd be a yellow ring
left by a mug of turmeric tea
you spat out and spluttered
to its bitter end.
It made you reach down
for the Skittle I didn't know
was stuck in my pocket
because you know
every soft corner of me,
every stained edge
and every skilled shape I make
in gold.

If I were a mark
left in your memory
I'd be a yellow ring
left by a mug of turmeric tea,
a blurred but stubborn boundary.

Sister

When they brought you home
in a wrinkly paper bag,
I tore you open like a gift
and pulled out
the mother in me.

Nine Years

For nine years
I had
an enormous belly.
It's still
a bit big
because
I can't bear
to think
you are no longer
in there.
Or anywhere.

The News

On Sugar Loaf Hill
the first snowdrops
speared the earth.
And word of my nephew's
first teeth spiking
through gums.
New life wrapped
in white velvet
and soft tissue.

Lullaby

We share the air,
shedding breath, speech, spit
into this public pool.

My song reaches yours
across the water,
its words drowning
somewhere in the middle

but I still know you
in ways which are mute
and flowing,
airways
mind-waves
soundscapes
whatever magic
you want to call it.

Circus

It's a wonky world
that hollows between
the winter and the spring;
a cross-pollination
of rot and revival.

The crocus births crooked
from pushing too hard and too soon,
choked by a mouthful of mulch
for its efforts, while

the snowdrops have grown heavy-
headed with grief,
crisp lines yielding to
parachutes — more flying
kisses than goodbyes.

Only the catkins remain
untouched by the pull of the soil,
swinging high in the trees
like acrobats looking down
at the clowns working the circus.

My whole life feels this distortion,
stretched between the bitter
and sweet air —
a tight rope tugged into a thread,
split into a hair,
Rootless
Rootless
Rootless

Sahara

Tears are stored in the hump
of my back...I was not born this way.

Grandmother perfectly preserved
in the smell of woodfire and jasmine.

Stray love spooning in
the hollow of a dimple.

Old selves that have disappeared
through the mirror.

Past lives clinging
to objects repurposed
in stranger's houses.

A tiny ghost buried
with the passing
of each month,
and many old ones exhumed
with the passing
of each year.

Oh God...
then there's the whole
pet cemetery.

I have more humps than a camel.

Guru

He came
in the form
of a stray furball
that scratched out
my heart,
and curled up

in the shape
of that space

and now I can see,
the sheep concentrated
in their camps.

Eulogy
All things bright and beautiful
All creatures great and small
All things wise and wonderful
The Lord God ate them all

Kākka the Crow

One of the first words
I learned to speak
was *crow*
which India Nana
taught me was *kākka*.
From then on
every crow was a friend
called Kākka the Crow.

On the day my mother's mother
died and every year since,
we cook her favourite foods
and place mouthfuls
on a deep green banana leaf
for the ravenous spirits
to fill their dark bellies.
This means that our ancestors
are remembered and well fed

and so the only grandparent
I ever knew, taught me
how to keep her alive
in my English garden.

Heirloom

It isn't an oversized brooch
demanding to be heard at a dinner party,
or an antique clock ticking off past lives
or an embroidered handkerchief —
initials unravelled to anonymity
by a vengeful nose, spraying and erasing
and designed to kill,
or a house passed down
rattling from the indigenous chatter of ghosts
with their books covered in dust and DNA.

It is life when I smell purple in the darkness,
the taste of exotic when ketchup dribbles down my chin,
the sound of belonging when I hear mother-on-the-tongue,
the cool simplicity of cotton content on my aching skin,
grace, when I see your face in the mirror...looming.

5th Beetle

'No Access'
It had come to this;
spurned by a
ten-inch laminated sign
which had my stage name on it.

I drove past this clotted wood
last Sunday,
had wanted to return all week.
Its darkness was so glossy
holding the promise
of a great black shell
to camouflage my own

but I must have cracked
somewhere, light slipping in
to make a little torch of me,
an intruder sent
to dim the mystery.

Nature is not stupid.

Lucky Dip

How life surprises you
at every twist and turn of her hips,
womb swaying between;
shaking all possibilities inside
like a baby tombola.

VI

Now I rain like a monsoon in Mayfair

Yellow Welly

It finally rained
a diamond
perfectly set in dirt,
reflecting the filth
speckled clouds
that snuffed out the sun,
dimmed the sparkle
I'd become.

Melted mirror ball
spreading into
crisp bags and
crushed cans of coke,
a flattened continuation of
no hope.

The rain, the skies
the storm in my eyes...

Glossy rabbit hole
waiting for Alice
to peer through
its illusion, broken
by a small yellow boot
and the realisation that

you can't walk on cloud nine,
any more than there is a heaven.

Heaven

The temple is ringing
through a thicket of traffic.
A call to 200 ankle bells
of all lengths and timbres
to gather either side of
the inner sanctum.

My hair is long
and tumbled with curls
from the waterlogged breeze,
flowing I imagine
like the Sarasvati River,
until redirected
with a feral tug from behind
by a stranger who tells me
to whirl it up in a bun, sharpish!
because God wouldn't
like to see me like that —
natural
comfortable
free and
easy.

I move to the back instead,
mangled between
ten ferocious armpits
that gas me
straight to hell anyway.

Black Stains

I know my darkness in the way
that light stains the glass
of sacred places
I want to sleep.

Hail Kali, wild disgrace, I am with thee.

There are many shades of black
that play behind my eyes set deep
in their sockets of lead
rimming round to seal in the night.

Hail Kali, wild disgrace, I am with thee.
Blessed art thou amongst women
and blessed is the fire in thy belly.

Fine Dining

It was lunchtime
at Grandmother's house.
The bottle of ketchup
we had brought with us
from England,
was proudly displayed
in the middle of the table.

We dipped our bread in it
like it was truffle oil
and talked about breasts
in the middle of *The Sun*
(that we didn't bring)
and how funny it was that
English girls were now wearing
bindis and brown boyfriends.

gingergarlic

ginger and garlic
are so commonly cooked together
that the mark of a good Indian chef
is to use neither.
Instead, more subtle flavours
must be favoured, such as fennel
and other fart tastes.

I don't see the problem.
I love gingergarlic —
in everything.
And it purifies the blood,
like a love-hate relationship
or when you love to hate
someone or something.

It purges all politeness
and decorum away,
things that hold you back
from saying what you really mean
and so are left
to burn and boil and curdle
in your veins.

Better then, to just use gingergarlic
because at least that way
there's no pressure
to earn five Malabar stars
or donate at a blood bank.
But please — we really don't need
another Gordon fkin' Ramsey.

Little India

Tangled snakes
sleep
behind the toaster.
One socket
Sixty plugs
that do not all lead
to Mecca.

Catnip

A hunt for the biscuit tin
in Mama's kitchen
may lead you to God.

The cupboard by the stove
is lined with candy stripes
once used to wrap the box set
of *Some Mothers Do 'Ave 'Em*;
now papered
around tiny figurines
of grease and gold.

Spirals of incense mingle
with the fumes from
tarka dhal or tomato soup;
blue flames dancing
their lunchtime ritual beneath
smoked steel.

Back in the cupboard
the lamp has gone out
and is smouldering
black rings on its Formica roof.

The shrine is in slumber —
Bagpuss on a rainy day.
How I still loved him...

Malabar Stars

The Backwaters lie
where fresh river water
sips the Arabian sea.
Untouched by swirling currents,
we are left to slide along the sky.
The only sound is of instinct
singing in my gut, soothed
between the song of
the egret and the cuckoo,
whose clock timed
my childhood in a
stagnant town in
Lancashire.

My internal compass
was spinning back then;
east-west-east-west-east-west,
trying to reroute
via smell, spice and sound
to a place that made sense
or at least felt safe.

Another houseboat races past.
Motorised half-naked Germans
in yellow bikinis and Speedos
cling on and wave with big teeth,
but I can hardly be bothered
to lift my holiday eyes.

When the salted edge finally appears —
fireworks prick the sky
bleeding lanterns in constellations
across the town, so I may see
where I have travelled
from the shores of Wigan Pier.

It is Christmas Day.

Bird's Eye

It was a very still day,
and the only thing moving
was the floater in my eye
which turned out to be
a high flying bird
pecking at a cloud.

Miles below I moved
like a dot on Google Maps
with no particular destination,
but zooming in I picked
out fine details on the ground...

If I had arrived ten seconds later
at the lake, I would have missed
two swans necklacing a heart

like on a greetings card
you don't know who to give.

On this day I might have
posted it to myself,
in celebration of
not being scared to dot the i's.

Wanderlust

When I finally
came home
to myself
I found
that my house
was not at all
in order.
And that
was the making
of me.

Chalai Bazaar

'To Chalai' said the sign
in two languages,
directing scores of
rickshaws to scatterbug
in ten different directions
like beetles caught naked
under a stone.

If you wear shorts here
you are also naked,
a skirt — also naked.
So I wore jeans
and a long top
to Chalai Bizarre
where you can buy
shorts and skirts
in different colours
including nude.

The market is teeming
with tourists,
so I rely on perfumed
instinct to navigate
the tangle of tiny lanes
that whip open their
trap doors on either side
to snatch my bangs
which are blunt,
so aren't going anywhere
except to the bangle shop
where they also sell headbands
in different colours
including black.

I left my fringe in Chalai Bazaar
I left my fringe in Chalai Bizarre
I left my fringe in Chalai Bazaar
La la la la la...

Sea Breeze

Ingredients:

50ml vodka
100ml cranberry juice
50ml freshly squeezed grapefruit
Ice
Thin slice of lime

Instructions:

1.Take a seat outside.
They will put you by the swimming pool
beneath the fingered palms
where a sitarist will later play tonight.
But ask for the table by the sea
where you can hear old songs
from its shells.

2. Order fried cutlets.
They will bring mango salsa or sauce,
but ask for the green chutney
that burns a rockpool to your tongue;
a taste of the coast rolling
all the way home.

3. Take a sip — go ahead, take a sip...
They will bring thin slices of lime.
Swap them for lychees —
buoys bobbing fleshy in a syrup of calm.
They will cut through the bitter and the sour
that swells like oceans inside you.

4. For the next round,
order a mocktail.
Just take out the vodka
and pretend you are a bird
sweetly calling out
your own bullshit.

5. Shake it up.
Don't be afraid.
Don't forget the ice.

*For a Cosmopolitan, swap
the grapefruit for Cointreau
and fuck off to Delhi.

Rani's Jubilee

Queen of hearts
Mother of pearls
Leader of women
Teacher of girls

Queen of hearts
Angel of doom
Daughter of heaven
Face of the moon

Queen of hearts
Painter of stars
Sculptress of rocks
Venus and Mars

Queen of hearts
Empress of seas
Priestess of love
The breath in the breeze

Queen of hearts
Why could I not see
I am Rani
Rani is me.

Pilgrimage

The sky sucked out my blue
and lit every shade of sadness
with a silver slash of sun.
Like a thousand midnight lamps
held on a pilgrimage back to self.

Traces

I carry my head like a snail
carries its home on its back,
spiralled skull-deep
into a sleep
that dreams of direction.

I too leave a silver trail.
The magical imprint
of me moving through the world
via song and poem
and stories from my different selves.

I can trace these twinkling lines
back in time to
constellations of thoughts.
Each thread as fine and bright
as a moonbeam guiding me back home.

Llyn Elsi

A steep climb
in slow reverse helter-skelter
up through the woods
and onto the lake crowning
the elevation.

Here she lay in state;
liquid gold, smelt
from the strong rays
of the sun.

We paid our respects,
resting on an overlooking bench
eating sandwiches as we watched
a variety of birds peck
into her wrinkling skin.

Someone threw a stone
but it could have been a jewel,
momentarily breaking
her kiss from the sky.

As the day deepened
the air began to hold its breath
allowing people to chant
their everyday lives and dreams
as they circled around her mouth.

I had an urge to throw in
a penny and make a wish
or at least a promise
to always flow like water,
so that I may finally
come to rest like this.

Closing Mantra

Blazing sun
Curse undone
See the spell
I've become

Rpt x 108

Appendix

Sleep will be the one
to shatter this sac
not on my back.
A dream of Gary Glittering
is really Semtex
spraying its swan song
in graffiti, yellow and green,
clogging the cogs
of my ticking machine.

I was only six when the surgeon
told me I nearly died
and prescribed something for
night terrors
day tremors
aches that would turn to years

then he took out the terrorist in my tummy
forgetting to leave its conviction
already rooted to the bone.
Hence forty odd years
not believing
I could do anything right.

Acknowledgements

'Black Grapes', 'My Regeneration', 'Jasmine', 'The Dandelion's Clock' and 'Camera Obscura' first appeared in *The Cannon's Mouth* magazine.

'The Gaze' first appeared in *Horses of a Different Colour* (Dempsey & Windle 2021).

In 'Holy Cows' I borrow some lyrics of Madonna's *Like a Prayer* and in 'Brown Girl in the Ring' I include some lyrics from Boney M's *Brown Girl in the Ring*. The borrowed lines are those in italics.

A HUGE thank you to:

Publishers Janice and Dónall Dempsey for your incredible support and making the creation of this book such a joyous and enjoyable process.

Callum James for selecting my poem The Gaze for the *Brian Dempsey Memorial Anthology* which led to the publication of this book.

Paul Windridge for all your help, advice and support over the years. I will always fondly remember our walk on Tennyson Down where you sparked my dream of writing this book into a reality.

Sharon Brooks for encouraging and inspiring me to write again. This is all your fault!

Karl Oldershaw for your generosity and help with the cover format.

My very talented fellow bandmates in Satsangi whom I have shared my songwriting journey.

My husband John Herbert for always believing in me and keeping the spirit of creativity alive every single day.

About the Author

Sujatha won her first poetry competition aged 8 with a poem about her father, a superhero and village doctor who used to visit his patients flying through the air in his 70's flares. However, to his disappointment she didn't follow in his footsteps and ran off to art school and joined a rock 'n' roll band instead. She has been song writing, recording and performing with the band Satsangi for 20 years and holds a 1st class honours degree and MA in the visual arts. By day she is a Holistic Health Practitioner and integrates poetry into her yoga classes and retreats.

For more information on Sujatha please visit:
www.sujathamenon.com

With very best wishes

Agatha x